HALLOWEEN
Holiday Grab Bag

by Judith Stamper

illustrated by Patrick Girouard

Troll Associates

METRIC EQUIVALENTS

1 inch = 2.54 centimeters
1 square inch = 6.45 square centimeters
1 foot = 30.5 centimeters

1 teaspoon = 5 milliliters (approx.)
1 tablespoon = 15 milliliters (approx.)
1 fluid ounce = 29.6 milliliters
1 cup = .24 liter
1 pint = .47 liter
1 quart = .95 liter
1 pound = .45 kilogram

Conversion from Fahrenheit to Celsius:
subtract 32 and then multiply the remainder by 5/9

LIBRARY OF CONGRESS CATALOGING-IN-PUBLICATION DATA
Stamper, Judith Bauer.
    Halloween holiday grab bag / by Judith Stamper; illustrated by Patrick Girouard.
        p.   cm.
    Summary: Discusses the origins of Halloween customs and suggests various activities for the holiday.
        ISBN 0-8167-2904-2 (lib. bdg.)   ISBN 0-8167-2905-0. (pbk.)
    1. Halloween decorations—Juvenile literature.   2. Halloween—Juvenile literature.   3. Cookery—Juvenile literature.   [1. Halloween.]
    I. Girouard, Patrick, ill.   II. Title.
    TT900.H32S73   1993
    745.594'1—dc20   92-13224

Contents

It's October 31! Halloween is here, and the spirit of magic has come alive. Witches, vampires, black cats, and monsters roam the streets. Ghost stories make us smile with delight — or shudder with fear.

How did this spooky holiday begin? For centuries before us, people have celebrated Halloween's magic. Many of their traditions are still with us today.

In ancient Scotland and Ireland, the Celtic peoples held a festival on October 31. This festival later became All Hallows' Eve — the day before All Hallows', or All Saints', Day. Evil spirits were said to roam the land on All Hallows' Eve. As the years went by, this night became known as Halloween.

People of long ago truly feared Halloween. They thought that dead people came back as ghosts. They thought witches flew on broomsticks. They thought the future could be read by magic omens.

Today, Halloween is still a time of fright. But most of all, it is a time of fun: a time for party games, grinning jack-o'-lanterns, and trick-or-treating.

The stories, crafts, recipes, and games in this book are all about Halloween. They will help make this holiday a special one for you.

J ck-O'-Lant rns

Jack-o'-lanterns give Halloween a special, spooky glow. Today, we set them in windows or on doorsteps to greet trick-or-treaters. But years ago, they were used as real lanterns.

People in Ireland and Scotland carved their jack-o'-lanterns out of turnips, potatoes, and beets. They carried them around with lighted candles inside. One legend says that the lanterns were named after a stingy old man named Jack. Now he was doomed to wander the earth forever with his lantern, because he was a miser.

When the Scots and the Irish came to America, they brought their Halloween tradition with them. And in North America, they found the best jack-o'-lantern of all — the pumpkin!

Carving the Pumpkin

1. Choose a pumpkin for your jack-o'-lantern. It can be big, little, fat, skinny, round, or bumpy. Each pumpkin will have its own special personality when it becomes a jack-o'-lantern.

2. Begin by making a lid for the pumpkin. With the help of an adult, cut out a star shape around the stem, making zigzag lines. Slant your knife in toward the center of the pumpkin. This will keep the lid from falling inside after it's cut.

3. Clean out the pumpkin until it is hollow. Save the seeds to use later on for a Halloween snack (see recipe on page 9).

4. Draw a face on your pumpkin with a pencil. Make eyes, a nose, and a mouth. You can also add eyebrows and uneven teeth. The pumpkin faces shown here may help to give you ideas. Decide if you want a happy face, a mean face, a spooky face, or a silly face. Again, with the help of an adult, carve out the face with a knife.

continued...

5. Set a candle inside the pumpkin to make it glow. With an adult's help, you can make a safe candle holder with a small, tin can like the sort that tuna comes in. Drip melted wax from your candle to the bottom of the can. Then stand up the candle in the wax. When the candle is lit, your pumpkin face will glow. Finally, put on the pumpkin's lid.

CANDLE

TIN CAN

TUNA·T

seeds

Your jack-o'-lantern is ready to shine for every ghost, goblin, witch, and monster on Halloween night!

Pumpkinseed Treat

The seeds you removed from your pumpkin make a tasty fall snack. And they're good for you, too!

1. Wash the seeds well.

2. Spread them out on a cookie sheet.

3. Sprinkle about 4 tablespoons of corn oil over the seeds. Add a little salt.

4. Bake in a 350°F oven for about fifteen minutes, or until light brown. (*Note:* If you're not allowed to use the oven by yourself, ask an adult for help.)

What do the birds sing on Halloween?

Twitch-or-tweet.

Why should a skeleton drink ten glasses of milk a day?

It's good for the bones.

What did the little ghost have in his rock collection?

Tombstones.

What do baby ghosts wear on Halloween?

White pillowcases.

What do you get when you drop a pumpkin?

Squash.

What do you call little black cats on Halloween?

Kittens.

Why did the witches' team lose the baseball game?

Their bats flew away.

BOO!

What was the witch's favorite subject in school?

Spelling.

The Witch's Night

On Halloween night, the witch flies through our imaginations on her broomstick. She wears a black cape and a black, pointed hat. Her hair is stringy, her face is ugly, and her black cat is by her side.

Our myths about the Halloween witch come from people who used to practice witchcraft long ago. The word *witch* means "wise one" or "magician." Superstitious people believed witches had many magical powers.

Witches brewed magic potions to make people fall in love. They cast magic spells to bring people under their power. They had magic rituals that seemed to make them fly. People of long ago feared the witches — especially when they gathered together on Halloween night!

BLACK PAPER

EYE OF NEWT

MAKEUP

GLUE

trick or treat

SCARY MASK

It's easy to pretend you're a witch on Halloween night. Visit a costume shop for a pointed black hat and a long black cape. Or make your own costume! Any piece of black material that's large enough to wrap around yourself will do for a cape. (You might want to sew on a hook-and-eye or a button and buttonhole to keep it closed. Ask a grownup to help if you're not very good at sewing.) And you can make a hat out of a couple of pieces of black construction paper. Fold one piece into a cone and tape the edges together. Then cut a ring out of a second piece and glue it to the bottom of the cone to make a brim for your hat.

If you want to look like a scary witch, you have to make your face look spooky, too. Buy a creepy mask to wear, or use makeup to change yourself into the strangest, scariest witch ever! Then head out into the night and do some haunting!

The Fortuneteller

Witches of long ago claimed to have many magic powers. One was being able to tell the future. Fortunetelling has always been popular at Halloween. Would you like to be a fortuneteller? You can amaze your friends with this simple trick.

Materials
Lemon juice
Pieces of paper
Brush
Lamp with a light bulb of approximately 100 watts.

Preparation
Dip your brush into the lemon juice. Write some letters and numbers on each slip of paper. The lemon "ink" dries invisibly. Each of these "codes" will be interpreted by you later as you read your friends' fortunes. For example, the letter "A" could be interpreted as the first initial of a future husband or as the first letter of a future job.

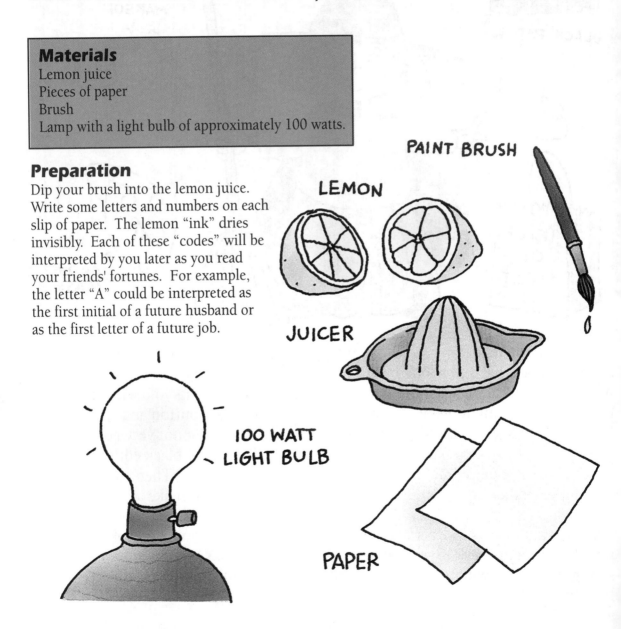

PAINT BRUSH

LEMON

JUICER

100 WATT
LIGHT BULB

PAPER

The Trick

Invite several friends to your house for a fortunetelling session. This trick is fun to do at Halloween parties, too.

Sit down over your crystal ball (the lamp with the burning light bulb). If the light bulb is too bright for your eyes, you might want to wear sunglasses. Choose one person and one piece of paper with an invisible "fortune." Hold the paper over the top of the light bulb. A minute later the fortune will appear — like magic! Now you can have the fun of interpreting the mysterious letter or number.

Why It Works

The lemon juice contains carbon. When heated, the carbon turns black or brown and makes the fortune appear.

Skeletons are part of the season's fright.
At Halloween, cemeteries become more scary.
Tombstones seem like bad omens.
And a grinning skeleton beckons eerily to us.

Your Hour Has Come
A Halloween Trick

Perform this trick for friends in a darkened room. You will need a clock with numbers on its face, a pencil, and a pad of paper. Choose an assistant who will point a flashlight at the clock.

Ask a person to come forward and pick an hour from one to twelve. Tell the player to write the number on a piece of paper and show it to the audience. You and your assistant must not see it.

Now explain that you will begin to tap on the clock's face with the pencil until you find the secret number. The player must silently count one number for each tap. Counting should begin with one number higher than the number chosen. When the player reaches *twenty,* he or she must shout it out loud.

You begin tapping. The first seven taps can fall anywhere on the clock's face. But the eighth tap must fall on number twelve. Then tap counterclockwise around the face (eleven, ten, nine, etc.) until the person shouts twenty.

To everyone's amazement, the pencil will be pointing to the chosen hour.

In a spooky voice, say "Your hour has come!" At that moment, have your assistant turn off the flashlight for a spooky effect. Shrieks and giggles will follow!

Halloween comes at the height of apple-harvest time. Crisp, juicy apples are perfect to use for many of the holiday's games and recipes. Here are some favorites. Try them at your next Halloween party.

Bobbing for Apples

Fill a low, wide tub two thirds full of water. Drop in ten to twenty apples of medium size. Each person tries to grab an apple between his or her teeth — before it bobs away!

Apple bobbing can be made even more fun with several tricks. Carve an initial in the bottom of each apple. Then predict that each person who gets an apple will marry someone with the initials shown on the apple. Or write up fortunes and tape them to the bottoms of the apples with clear tape (cover the fortunes completely to make them waterproof).

Apple-Seed Fortune

Carefully cut an apple open and sort out the seeds. Count how many there are.

Two seeds predict good luck.

Three predict bad luck.

Four predict wealth.

Five predict early marriage.

Six predict fame.

Seven predict a great surprise in the near future!

continued...

Caramel Apples

You Will Need

6 medium apples
1 pound caramel candies
2 tablespoons water
6 ice-cream sticks

Tablespoon
Saucepan
Wooden spoon
Wax paper
Potholder

Steps

1. Push a stick into each apple.

2. Combine the caramel candies and the water in the saucepan. Heat over low heat. Use a wooden spoon to stir into a smooth mixture. (Note: If you're not allowed to use the stove by yourself, ask an adult for help.)

3. Using a potholder, remove the pan from the stove. Dip the apples into the caramel, covering them completely.

4. Set the apples on wax paper. Put them in the refrigerator to cool and harden. Then enjoy!

The Golden Cane

A Scary Story for You to Tell

This story should be told in a dark room or around a campfire at night. Choose at least two or three other people to be your audience...or victims.

Long ago, there lived a stingy, mean old man. One day, the man's leg was hurt in an accident. He was too proud to use a wooden cane. So he took all his savings and bought a cane of pure gold! His wife, who never had anything, looked at the cane with envy.

Years later, the old man died. And when his will was read, his wife had a shock. The man had written that his golden cane must be buried with him!

continued...

The idea of keeping the valuable cane for herself began to haunt the woman. The night before her husband was buried, she couldn't sleep at all. At midnight, she slipped out of bed, climbed down the staircase, and went to the coffin. She opened the lid, grabbed the golden cane, and ran back to her room.

Night after night, while she slept, the woman dreamed of the money she would get for the golden cane. But one night, her dreams were interrupted. She woke with a start.

Outside, the wind was howling and moaning. And over the wind, a voice spoke to her.

"Whooooooooo...whoooooooo stole my golden cane?"

The woman ran to the windows and locked the shutters tight. She barred the door. Then she jumped back in bed and covered her head with the blankets.

continued...

But the voice came again, closer and louder.

"*Whooooo...whooooo* stole my golden cane? *Whooooo?*"

The woman heard a door creak open downstairs. She began to tremble and quiver.

The voice crept up the stairway now.

"*Whooooo...whooooo* stole my golden cane? *Whooooo? Whooooo?*"

Then the bedroom door flew open. An icy draft swept into the room. The woman crouched under the blankets, her heart pounding. Then the voice came again...this time in a whisper...in her ear!

"Whooooo...whooooo stole my golden cane? *Whooooo?"*

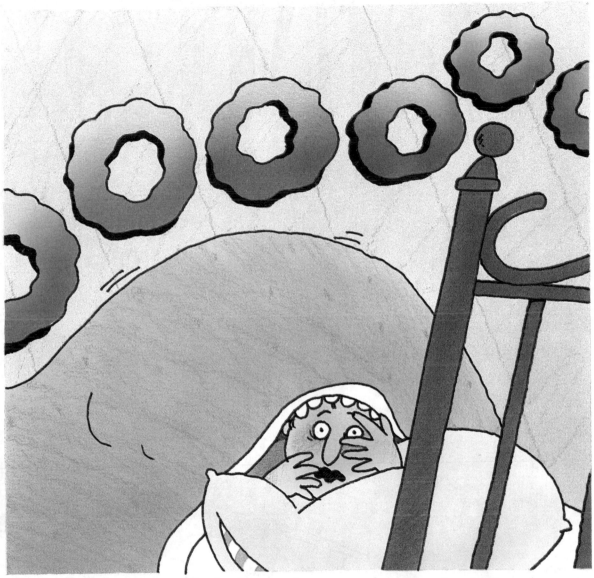

Stop telling the story suddenly. Turn to the person next to you and ask "What happens next?"

Make a game out of finishing the story. Ask everyone in the circle to add his or her own ending. See *whoooo* can make up the spookiest ending to the story.

How to Tell If a House Is
HAUNTED

Checklist

Banging shutters
Bats
Black cat on porch
Broken window
Cemetery in back yard
Clock stopped at midnight
Cobwebs
Coffin in living room
Creaking staircase
Flickering candle
Full moon overhead
Ghost in attic
Mice
Piano playing by itself
Scream from basement
Thumping noises on stairs
Werewolf in bushes
Witch in kitchen

Haunted-House Fun

Here's a party idea for some Halloween fun. Make your own haunted house —
at home. The ideas below will give you a start. Add to them by letting your
imagination go *wild*.

1. *Pick a room* in your house
to be the chamber of horrors. A
basement would work, or even
your own bedroom. Be sure the
room can be made pitch dark.

2. *Make a tunnel of terror* for
your visitors to go through.
Connect large, cardboard boxes to
make the tunnel. Or set up several
small card tables and drape them
with sheets. Or drape the sheets over
a long rope and secure them tent-
style at the bottom.

3. *Hang creepy creatures* from the top of the tunnel. Dangle rubber spiders from strings. Let a damp mop rub against your visitors' heads. Fill a rubber glove with cold water, tie off the top, and let it caress each visitor's face in the dark.

4. *Paste scary, black cut-outs* on the outside of the sheets or cut out scary shapes in the cardboard boxes. Shine a flashlight on the cut-outs. Then turn the light on and off for a scary effect.

5. *Play a tape recording* of spooky sounds. You may be able to find a Halloween tape in your local library. Better yet, make your own soundtrack. Include ghostly howling, screams, rattling chains, clumping feet, cackling voices, and the sound of thunder.

AWOOOOOOO
EEEEEEK
ARGHHHHHHHH

continued...

6. *Test your visitors' courage* at the end of the tunnel. In the dark, dare them to put their hands in a witch's brew. Fill a plastic bucket with slimy foods: cold, oily spaghetti; small pickles; peeled onions; and so on.

PICKL

PEARL ONIONS

OIL

7. *Make scary predictions* about the future for each person. Pretend that you are a wicked witch or wizard.

8. *Release your visitors* from the chamber of horrors with a final, loud howl!

YOU WILL KISS A FROG!

Skeletons

The Inside Story

Did you know that the amazing human skeleton has over two hundred bones? Some are large, like the thighbone. Others are small, like the 27 bones in your hand. Look at this drawing of a skeleton. Can you feel each bone in your own body that is shown in the picture?

Bats are as creepy as Halloween itself. By night, they swoop through the air, searching for prey. By day, they hang upside down, their wings folded around them like a witch's cape. And where do they hang around? Caves, castles, and especially haunted houses!

Vampires and Vampire Bats

Horror movies pair the bat with another creepy creature — the vampire. In fact, Count Dracula and the bat have a lot in common. The bat spreads its dark wings just as the vampire spreads his black cape. And if you look at their faces, you'll see the Count and the bat share the same, sharp smile — with the same spiky, pointed teeth.

Not all bats have the appetite of Count Dracula. But the vampire bats of Central America are, in fact, bloodsuckers. These bats weigh only one ounce, but have a wingspan of about twelve inches. Cattle are their main victims, although human beings have also been bitten. The vampire bat bites a chunk out of its victim's skin, licks the blood from the wound, and then flies away. Each small bat drinks about one tablespoon of blood per day. Luckily, vampire bats aren't the largest bats!

Witches and Bats

Like a black cat, the bat is a witch's best friend. Long ago, bats were often part of superstitious rituals. A witch watched a bat's movements to foretell the future. And any proper witch's brew contained a bat wing, a bat tooth, or a bat heart.

Bat Facts

Bats are not blind. All species can see, but many have poor eyesight.

Most bats are harmless, but wild bats may carry rabies.

All bats are not black. They may be brown, gray, yellow, or red.

The largest bat has a wingspan of five feet.

The bat is the only flying mammal.

Bats fly in the dark by sending out high-pitched sounds. Echoes bouncing back help them navigate through the darkness.

Ghastly Giggles

Why did the mummy call the doctor?

Because he was coffin.

What does a vampire fear most?

Tooth decay.

Where did the vampire open his savings account?

At a blood bank.

What did the mad scientist eat on Halloween?

Frankenfurters with ketchup.

Where do mummies go for a swim?

To the Dead Sea.

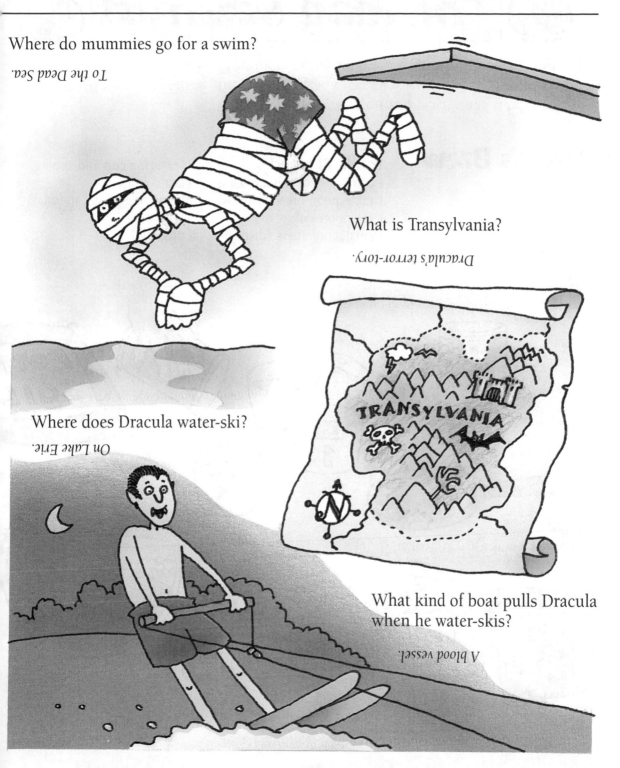

What is Transylvania?

Dracula's terror-tory.

Where does Dracula water-ski?

On Lake Erie.

What kind of boat pulls Dracula when he water-skis?

A blood vessel.

The Mad Scientist

Dr. Frankenstein created a monster in his laboratory. Would you like to be a mad scientist, too? Try this science experiment in your home laboratory — the kitchen. You'll get a trick, but no treat!

Witch's Brew

You Will Need

1 can celery or tomato soup
1 tablespoon bread crumbs
1 teaspoon soil
3 small containers (disposable, if possible)

Measuring cup and spoons
Plastic wrap
Magnifying glass (optional)

Steps

1. Pour 1/2 cup undiluted soup into each container.

2. In the first container, sprinkle the bread crumbs.

3. In the second container, sprinkle bits of soil.

4. For the third container, first, run your finger across a dusty or dirty surface. Then dip your finger into the soup.

5. Seal all containers with plastic wrap. Store them in a dark, warm place for three days.

6. Pull out your witch's brew and uncover. Surprise! What are those strange things growing on top?

Why It Happens

Your witch's brew is really a garden of mold. Mold is an unusual type of plant. It grows by feeding off living or dead plant or animal substances. The mold in your containers is living off the soup.

How did it get there? The bread crumbs, soil, and your dusty finger contained mold spores. When the spores are given nourishment, moisture, warmth, and darkness, they grow into the strange, colorful molds on the soup.

Inspect the mold with a magnifying glass. If you like, you can read more about mold in an encyclopedia.

Halloween Trivia Quiz

What are the two colors of Halloween?

Black and orange.

In which village did the Headless Horseman chase Ichabod Crane?

Sleepy Hollow.

Where did the famous witch trials of New England take place?

Salem, Massachusetts.

What is a group of witches called?

A coven.

What kind of signs are painted on the barns of the Pennsylvania Dutch to ward off witches and bad luck?

Hex signs.

In what country were real mummies made?

Egypt.

How many bones are in the human skeleton?

Over 206.

When are werewolves said to come out?

During a full moon.

What is worn around the neck to keep away vampires?

Garlic.

Some children trick-or-treat for UNICEF. What does UNICEF stand for?

United Nations International Children's Emergency Fund.

A Ghostly Game

The game of Ghost may be played by two or more people. The first player names a letter of the alphabet. The second player thinks of a word beginning with that letter and adds a second letter. The next player must think of a word beginning with these two letters and adds a third letter. The object of the game is to add on a letter that continues the spelling of a word — but does not finish the word.

Rules

1. Any player who ends a word on the third letter or after becomes a "half-ghost."

2. When a player becomes a half-ghost twice, he or she becomes a "whole ghost." That's the time to disappear from the game!

3. Any player may challenge another to say the word he or she has in mind after adding a letter. If the player can't name the word, he gets a half-ghost penalty. If the player does name the word, the challenger gets a half-ghost penalty.

4. Continue playing the game until only one player is left — the winner. The ghosts are the losers.

Are you up-to-date on your monster history? Here are some interesting facts and legends about some ghastly ghouls.

The Mummy

Did You Know?

The ancient Egyptians buried their dead leaders in magnificent tombs. When these tombs were opened centuries later, the bodies of the dead were found as mummies.

They were preserved and wrapped in strips of fine white linen.

These ancient mummies became the source of great superstition. Many people believed in the mummy's curse: Revenge upon whoever opens the coffin of a mummy!

The Vampire

Did You Know?

In Eastern Europe, superstitious people lived in fear of the blood-thirsty vampire. The vampire, it was believed, rose from his grave at night to drink the blood of the living. The victim's fate was to die and rise again — as a vampire!

Count Dracula is the most famous vampire in books and movies. He has sharp fangs and horrible, staring eyes.

According to superstition, a vampire can be killed only one way — by driving a stake through his heart.

continued...

The Werewolf

Did You Know?

All over the world, people used to believe in shape-shifters. These were human beings who could change into animals. In Europe, the most infamous shape-shifter was a werewolf.

The werewolf had a man's body, but the furry features of a wolf. It prowled about at night doing evil deeds — especially during a full moon!

The Zombie

Did You Know?

The myth of the walking dead comes from Africa and Haiti. A zombie is a corpse that has been given life again through magic. With a dead-looking face, the zombie walks about like a robot. Legend portrays the zombies as wearing chains because they are the slaves of their evil masters.

Pass the Corps

This Halloween game will send shivers down the spines of even your bravest friends. Arrange chairs in a circle for everyone to sit down. Play the game at night or in a room that can be made pitch dark.

Announce to your friends that you have just returned from a cemetery — with a corpse! Then, one at a time, pass small bowls around the circle. Each will contain these parts of the corpse:

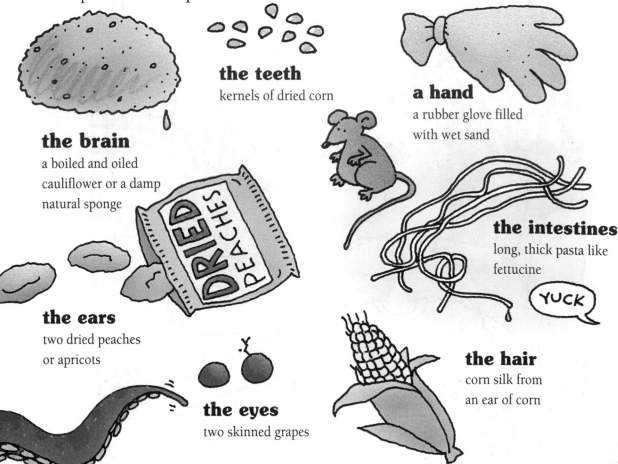

the teeth
kernels of dried corn

the brain
a boiled and oiled cauliflower or a damp natural sponge

a hand
a rubber glove filled with wet sand

the intestines
long, thick pasta like fettucine

YUCK

the ears
two dried peaches or apricots

the eyes
two skinned grapes

the hair
corn silk from an ear of corn

In a dramatic voice, tell your friends to be quiet and listen. Jangle some chains and moan, or have an accomplice do it in the background. Announce in a creepy voice that it is the corpse's spirit — coming for revenge!

Turn on the lights suddenly and let everyone see each other's frightened face.

Twenty Top Costume Ideas

Black cat
Devil
Fortuneteller/gypsy
Ghost
Monster
Movie star
Mummy
Nerd
Outer-space creature
Pirate
Pumpkin
Robot
Rock star
Skeleton
Super-hero or super-heroine
Vampire or vampirella
Werewolf
Witch
Wizard
Zombie

Trick-or-Treat Tips

 Daylight is the safest time to trick-or-treat.

 At night, carry a flashlight and wear reflective tape on your costume.

 Never trick-or-treat alone. Travel in groups and with an adult, if possible.

 Be sure your costume is safe to walk in.

 Don't wear a mask that blocks part of your vision.

 Walk on well-lighted streets.

 Cross streets only at corners.

 Tell your parents your route.

 Check your treats with an adult at home before eating them.